Unlocking Integrity-Centered Leadership

UNLOCKING INTEGRITY-CENTERED LEADERSHIP

Be Good. Do Good. Do Well.

Gopu Shrestha

Senior Agile Coach | Author | Leadership Speaker

strategichonesty.com

Strategic Honesty Publishing

Blaine, Minnesota

Copyright © 2025 Gopu Shrestha
All rights reserved.

No part of this publication may be reproduced, distributed, or transmitted in any form or by any means, including photocopying, recording, or other electronic or mechanical methods, without the prior written permission of the publisher, except in the case of brief quotations embodied in critical reviews and certain other noncommercial uses permitted by copyright law.

Published by Strategic Honesty Publishing
Blaine, Minnesota
strategichonesty.com

First Edition
Printed in the United States of America

To my sons,

and to my beautiful wife—whose unwavering support, honest guidance, and steady belief in my mission have carried me through every season of this journey. Thank you for keeping our boys connected to the purpose behind my work, so they grow up understanding not just what their father does, but why he does it.

To my mentors, colleagues, Toastmasters friends, and coaches— thank you for shaping my growth, challenging my thinking, and standing beside me in the shared commitment to help others rise through the power of leadership and learning.

This book is as much yours as it is mine.

How to Read This Book

You picked up this book for a reason. Maybe you are navigating a difficult decision at work. Maybe you are raising children and wondering how to teach them what really matters. Maybe you feel the pull between doing what is easy and doing what is right, and you are not sure which path to take.

Whatever brought you here — welcome. This book was written for you.

Unlocking Integrity-Centered Leadership is not a collection of theories or corporate talking points. It is a memoir in disguise, a field guide dressed up as a leadership book, written by someone who has lived every principle on these pages — sometimes painfully, sometimes triumphantly, and always honestly.

The best way to use this book:

Start with the Preface. It is short, but it sets the tone for everything that follows. It tells you who I am, where I came from, and why I believe so deeply in what you are about to read.

Then, you have two paths. If you have time, read from Chapter 1 through Chapter 38. The book is built as a journey — each part deepens the one before it. You will move from inner work to daily practice to complex decisions to lasting legacy.

If life is busy — and whose is not? — jump directly to the chapter that speaks to your current challenge. Are you struggling with self-doubt or a crisis of values? Start with Part I. Do you want to strengthen trust and daily leadership? Go to Part II. Facing a gray-area ethical situation? Part III is for you. Ready to put everything into practice and build something lasting? That is Part IV.

However you read it, I ask one thing: do not just read. Pause. Reflect. Ask yourself the questions tucked inside these chapters. The power of this book is not in the words — it is in what you do after you close it.

My journey took me from a kerosene-lit village in Nepal, where I studied by dim light and dreamed of a different life, to the boardrooms and volunteer halls of America. If that journey taught me one unshakeable truth, it is this:

> *Where you start does not determine where you lead. Your character does.*

Thank you for being here. Now let us begin.

— Gopu Shrestha

Blaine, Minnesota

Preface

I never expected my life to become a leadership story.

I grew up in a village in rural Nepal where there was no electricity, no running water, and no road connecting us to the wider world. At night, my family gathered under the faint glow of a kerosene lamp. We cooked over wood fire. The future felt distant, uncertain, and often heavy.

And yet, even as a boy sitting cross-legged on a mud floor, I held onto something stubborn inside me — a belief that if I stayed honest, if I kept doing the right thing even when no one was watching, somehow, somehow, things would open up. I could not articulate it then. I just knew it felt true.

That belief was tested many times. The first real test came when I borrowed money from a friend just to learn how to type. I was a young man with a secondary school education, a big family depending on me, and very few options. Within five years, that one small act of commitment carried me to a position in an international organization, earning ten times the average income from my village. But the salary was secondary. What I earned that mattered more was something money cannot buy: a reputation for honesty.

There was a moment, early in my career, when two managers went to war with each other over an ego dispute. Both of them wanted me to choose a side. I was the administrative assistant — I knew all the documents, all the facts, all the truth. Choosing sides would have been easy. It might even have helped my career in the short term. But I refused. My boss turned against me. I missed promotions. I watched others advance while I held still.

I held still for seven years.

And then something shifted. The people who had watched me hold still through all of it — they were the ones who eventually called me trustworthy. Not the managers who had demanded loyalty. The ones who had simply watched.

> *Integrity is not what you do when people are watching. It is what you do when they are not.*

This book is the result of decades of living that truth — as an immigrant, as a volunteer leader, as a professional, as a father, and as a coach. It is not a theory. It is a field guide, written from the trenches of real life, for anyone who wants to lead in a way that actually lasts.

You will find 38 chapters here, organized into four parts. Part I builds the foundation — who you are, what you value, and why it matters. Part II moves into the daily disciplines that earn trust. Part III takes you into the harder terrain of complexity, ambiguity, and pressure. Part IV is where everything becomes action — the decisions, the relationships, and the legacy.

This book is not for perfect people. It is for real people who feel the tension between what is easy and what is right. If that is you — this book was written for you.

> *When you lead with integrity, you do not just build a career. You build something that outlasts you.*

Welcome to the journey.

— Gopu Shrestha

Blaine, Minnesota

Contents

How to Read This Book   vii
Preface   ix

PART I — Foundations of Integrity-Centered Leadership

1. Aligning Personal Values for Long-Term Satisfaction and Success   3
2. Embracing Challenges for Personal Growth   6
3. Crafting Your Identity and Taking Ownership   8
4. Learning from Role Models and Mentors   10
5. Building a Strong Reputation and Legacy   12
6. Crafting an Authentic Personal Brand   14
7. Strategic Honesty: The Cornerstone of Leadership   16
8. Character and Integrity Amidst Adversity   18
9. Unlocking the Power of Truth and Transparency   20
10. Innovative Solutions Through Honesty   22

PART II — Core Principles of Integrity-Centered Leadership

11. Humility: A Pathway to Leadership Excellence   25
12. Work Ethics: The Bridge from Poverty to Prosperity   27
13. Transforming Challenges into Opportunities   29
14. Accountability and Growth through Mistakes   31
15. Integrity in Personal Brand Building   33
16. From Foe to Friend: Turning Adversaries into Allies   34

PART III — Advanced Concepts in Integrity-Centered Leadership

17. Authenticity Over False Branding   37
18. Sustainable Success: Rejecting Get-Rich-Quick Thinking   39

19. Wealth Through Purpose and Fulfillment ... 41
20. Transforming Failure into Positive Change ... 43
21. Making Informed Decisions Through Clarity ... 45
22. Cultivating Self-Honesty and Growth ... 47
23. Avoiding Self-Sabotage Through Integrity ... 49
24. Integrity as a Spiritual Practice ... 51
25. Envisioning Your Future Self with Integrity ... 52
26. Investing in Emotional Integrity and Trust ... 54

PART IV — Integrity in Action

27. Commitment to Your Path of Integrity ... 57
28. Making Amends and Restoring Integrity ... 59
29. Leveraging Credibility for Protection ... 61
30. Utilizing Credibility for Positive Impact ... 63
31. Treating Others Well: The Ethical Imperative ... 65
32. Safeguarding Your Unshakeable Integrity ... 67
33. Honoring Commitments and Building Trust ... 69
34. Presenting Yourself as a Trustworthy Leader ... 71
35. Unlimited Credibility: A Continuous Pursuit ... 73
36. Failure as a Steppingstone to Achievement ... 75
37. Seeking Enlightening Feedback for Growth ... 77
38. Persistence and the Richness of Long-Term Payoffs ... 79

References ... 81

About the Author ... 83

PART I

Foundations of Integrity-Centered Leadership

Everything begins with who you are when no one is watching. Before you can lead others, you have to know yourself — your values, your story, your wounds, and your strengths. Part I is about that foundation. It is the inner work that makes the outer work possible.

CHAPTER 1
Aligning Personal Values for Long-Term Satisfaction and Success

There is a version of success that looks good on paper but feels hollow inside. I have seen it. Professionals who climb every rung of the ladder and arrive at the top feeling strangely empty. Parents who provide everything material and still wonder if they have given their children what matters most.

What is missing, in most cases, is alignment. When your daily choices do not match what you actually believe in, there is a kind of quiet friction that never quite goes away. You feel it in small moments — when you hesitate before speaking in a meeting, when you go through the motions of a job that stopped meaning anything, when you give your children advice you yourself do not follow.

I know that friction well.

The Moment That Changed Everything

I was a young man from a poor rural background with only a secondary education when I decided I wanted to become a highly paid professional. Looking at where I started, that ambition seemed nearly impossible. But I was determined to find a way.

I borrowed money from a friend to take typing classes, believing that becoming a typist could change my future. That is it. That was my strategy — one skill, one door. Within five years, I had secured a position as an officer in an international organization, earning ten times what the average person from my village earned.

But here is what I want you to hear: it was not just the typing that changed my life. It was the decision underneath the typing — the decision to invest in myself, to align what I was doing with what I wanted to become. The skill opened the door. The value underneath it built the foundation.

> *Reflect:* What is one thing you are doing every day that contradicts who you want to become? What would it look like to change that?

How Your Values Shape Your Relationship with Wealth

We talk a great deal about success, but we rarely slow down to ask: success according to whom? In my village, a successful man provided food for his family. In America, success often means status and salary. Neither definition is wrong — but neither is complete.

Real, lasting satisfaction comes when you get clear on what you actually value and then build a life that reflects those values. Not the values your parents wanted for you, not the values your culture assigns, but the ones you find when you sit quietly and ask: what is it that I am really here to do?

For me, that answer has always come back to one word: integrity. Not because integrity is fashionable. But because every time I compromised it, even slightly, I felt it. And every time I held to it — even when it cost me — I felt steady.

When Staying True Has a Price

I want to tell you about a period in my career that I do not talk about often, because it was painful and because it does not make me look like a hero. Two managers in my organization were fighting each other over a dispute rooted in nothing but ego. Both of them came to me — I was the administrative assistant, I knew where all the documents were, I knew who was right and who was wrong.

Both of them wanted me to choose their side.

I refused. I stayed honest. And my direct supervisor, who had wanted me firmly in his corner, turned against me. I did not get promoted for years. I watched colleagues advance while I stayed in the same position, doing good work that seemed invisible.

But I stayed for seven years. And when I finally left, my supervisor — the same one who had quietly worked against me — wrote me one of the best recommendations I have ever received. He told me later that he had been watching me the entire time.

People are always watching, even when it feels like no one is.

Selecting the Right Environment

One thing I have learned that rarely gets discussed in leadership books: your environment shapes you more than your willpower does. I grew up surrounded by poverty and limited expectations. Had I stayed inside that environment without actively seeking something different — without talking to my teachers, without borrowing that money to learn typing — I might have accepted those limits as my own.

Jim Collins writes in Good to Great about the importance of getting the right people on the bus before you decide where the bus is going. I believe the same principle applies to your personal life. Before you set your goals, look at who you are spending your time with. Are they people who share your values? People who stretch you, who call you up rather than down?

Ambitions that are not nurtured by the right environment tend to wither quietly. The right environment does not give you ambition — it keeps it alive.

> **Reflect:** *Who around you brings out your best self? Who quietly dims your sense of what is possible?*

Aligning your values with your daily choices is not a one-time decision. It is a practice. Some days you will get it exactly right. Other days, you will notice the gap between who you are and who you want to be. That gap is not failure — it is information. Use it.

CHAPTER 2

Embracing Challenges for Personal Growth

In 1989, when I started my information technology career, some of my colleagues were terrified of computers. Many believed the machines would cost them their livelihoods. They avoided learning computers or any new technology, holding on to manual work even as it faded away. I understood their fear — change can feel like a threat before it reveals itself as a gift.

Fast forward to today. The children of those colleagues are software engineers. What their parents feared became the very thing that opened new futures for the next generation.

That is what challenges do, when you let them.

The Two Mindsets That Define Everything

Carol Dweck, in her landmark book Mindset, describes two ways of moving through the world. A fixed mindset treats intelligence and ability as static — you either have it or you do not, and failure means you do not. A growth mindset believes abilities are developed through effort, learning, and persistence — and failure means you have not yet arrived.

I have met people from both camps throughout my life. The ones who struggled most were rarely the ones with the least talent. They were the ones who believed their limitations were permanent.

The ones who surprised everyone — including themselves — were the ones who stayed curious when things got hard.

> **Reflect:** *Think of a challenge you are facing right now. What would it look like to approach it with genuine curiosity instead of resistance?*

When the Threat Becomes the Gift

Change is uncomfortable because it asks us to let go of something familiar before we know what comes next. That gap — between the familiar and the unknown — is where most people stop.

But it is also where growth lives.

I went from typist to computer operator to computer engineer. I built three master's degrees — not all at once, not easily, but steadily. Each transition required me to walk through that uncomfortable gap. Each time, I had to believe that what was on the other side was worth the discomfort of not yet knowing.

John Maxwell writes in The 21 Irrefutable Laws of Leadership that leadership is a continuous growth and development journey. I have found that to be true in every domain of life, not just in the professional one. The parents who grow are the ones who remain open. The leaders who grow are the ones who stay teachable.

Leading Teams Through Change

Some years ago, I led a team through a significant shift — moving our software development approach from a waterfall to an agile approach. Human nature resists change, and this was no exception. Some team members had been doing things the same way for twenty years. They were not resistant out of stubbornness; they were resistant out of loyalty to what had worked.

Before I told anyone what to do, I started by telling them the truth. Our shared goal was simple: reduce defects by one percent and deliver better software on time. I worked alongside the team every single day. I did not hide our progress or our setbacks. I made asking for help the norm, not the exception.

The change happened slowly, then all at once. And when it did, the team owned it — because they had been part of it from the beginning.

Challenges do not weaken us by accident. They strengthen us by design — if we let them. The question is never whether challenges will come. The question is what you will do with them when they arrive.

CHAPTER 3
Crafting Your Identity and Taking Ownership

There is a concept I return to often, drawn from Jocko Willink and Leif Babin's Extreme Ownership: true leaders take complete responsibility for everything that happens under their watch. No excuses. No blame. No deflection.

When I first encountered that idea, I felt the weight of it. It is a demanding way to live. But I also felt the freedom in it — because if you are responsible for everything, then you are also empowered to change everything.

Who Are You When No One Is Defining You?

Identity is something most of us inherit before we choose it. The values of our families, the expectations of our cultures, the stories people tell about us before we are old enough to tell our own — all of it shapes who we believe ourselves to be.

At some point, though, life asks you to step into the work of choosing your identity intentionally. Who do you want to be? Not in broad, abstract terms, but in the specific moments that test your character — when you are tired, when you are under pressure, when no one would know the difference if you cut a corner?

That is where identity is built. Not in the declarations. In the daily choices.

Leadership Is About Others, Not Yourself

When I was an Area Director in Toastmasters, I noticed that some members had been working toward a specific award — the Distinguished Toastmaster title — for fifteen or twenty years without achieving it. I had reached that milestone in a decade, which gave me some insight into what made the difference.

I shared everything I knew. I gave members opportunities to practice. I stayed available. And the people I supported during that time became more than colleagues — they became lifelong friends. One of them became my co-leader at the district level, and together we earned the President's Distinguished Recognition.

Here is what I learned: when you invest in others without keeping score, the return is not just better outcomes. It is a different kind of relationship — the kind built on genuine trust.

Owning Your Mistakes as a Leader

Taking ownership of your mistakes is not weakness. It is the strongest signal of leadership I know.

During my tenure as District Director, I made decisions that not everyone agreed with. There were times I misjudged situations and times I moved too quickly. When I recognized those moments, I said so directly. I did not wait for someone else to name it first.

The leaders I most admired never blamed their teams when things went wrong. They asked, What did I miss? What could I have done differently? That question, asked sincerely, is worth more than any apology.

> *Reflect: Where in your life are you still waiting for someone else to take responsibility for something you could own yourself?*

Your identity is not fixed. It is built — choice by choice, day by day, in the moments when it would be easier to look the other way. Own those moments, and you own your story.

CHAPTER 4

Learning from Role Models and Mentors

When I was about twenty-seven years old, I found myself thinking seriously about the future — not just the next year, but the next decade. Who did I want to be in ten years? What kind of person was I working toward?

I looked around at the people in my life and started paying attention differently. Instead of seeing colleagues, I started seeing teachers. One man stood out. My supervisor. He had achieved things I admired — not just professionally, but personally. He carried himself with a kind of quiet authority that came from somewhere real.

Without ever telling him, I chose him as my mentor. And without ever lecturing me, he taught me the most important things I know.

The Mentor Who Never Told Me What to Do

What made him exceptional was not that he had all the answers. It was that he never gave me answers he had not earned. He would ask questions. He would point me toward experiences rather than conclusions. When I came to him with a problem, he would often turn it back on me: What do you think you should do?

At first, that frustrated me. I wanted guidance, not homework. But over time, I realized what he was doing — he was building my confidence in my own judgment. He was teaching me to own my decisions rather than borrow his.

I have tried to be that kind of person for others ever since.

Why You Need More Than One Mentor

During my years as District Director, I maintained relationships with four or five mentors at any given time. Each one had different strengths, different blind spots, different experiences. Some were professionals. Some were community leaders. Some were older than me; some were younger.

No single person has all the wisdom you need for all the situations you will face. Different mentors offer different lights. And the more perspectives you carry, the less likely you are to navigate important decisions in the dark.

Role Models Beyond Your Immediate Circle

Steve Jobs attributed much of his leadership development to Bill Campbell, his coach. Oprah Winfrey has spoken movingly about the way Maya Angelou shaped her sense of self and purpose. These are not abstract examples — they are reminders that every person who has done something meaningful has, somewhere in their story, a person who believed in them before they believed in themselves.

You do not have to know your role models personally. Some of mine I have never met — I know them through their words and their work. Viktor Frankl's writing on meaning, Angela Duckworth's research on grit, James Clear's thinking on habits — all of it has shaped how I lead, how I parent, and how I think about my own life.

> *Reflect: Who are the two or three people — living or not, near or far — whose example you most want to carry into your own life? What specifically about them do you want to embody?*

The people you learn from become part of who you are. Choose them carefully. Seek them actively. And when you have received enough, become one for someone else.

CHAPTER 5

Building a Strong Reputation and Legacy

I have been thinking lately about a word we use too casually: legacy. We tend to reserve it for famous people — for presidents and inventors and famous athletes. But legacy is not something that happens after you die. It is something you are building right now, with every choice, every relationship, every moment of integrity under pressure.

Your reputation is the evidence. It is what people say when you are not in the room.

The Slow Architecture of Trust

Trust does not arrive all at once. It is built through small, consistent acts — showing up when you said you would, telling the truth when a lie would be more comfortable, holding someone's confidence when it would be easier to pass it along.

I spent seven years in a job where my direct supervisor was working against me. Seven years. People sometimes ask me how I stayed. I stayed because I knew my reputation was the one thing he could not take from me. He could block my promotions. He could create friction. What he could not do was change the way the rest of the organization saw me — because I had built that myself, one interaction at a time.

When it was finally time to leave, that reputation opened every door.

Aligning Who You Are with What You Stand For

Anita Roddick built The Body Shop not just as a business, but as a values declaration. Her reputation was inseparable from her principles — fair trade, environmental responsibility, human dignity. She did not just sell products; she sold a way of being in the world.

That kind of alignment — between who you are and what you stand for — is what creates legacy. It is not manufactured. It is not marketed. It grows from the inside out.

Abraham Lincoln's legacy endures not because he was powerful, but because he was honest in one of the hardest moments in American history. His integrity was the through-line.

Legacy Begins at Home

I think about my two sons often when I think about legacy. One served in the United States Army. The other is an Environmental Engineer. They chose those paths themselves — I did not push them toward either. But I believe the values I tried to live in front of them shaped who they became.

That is the part of legacy no one writes about in business books: the children who watch you. They notice everything. They notice whether you keep your promises. They notice whether you treat people differently based on whether they can do anything for you. They notice whether the person you are at work and the person you are at home are the same person.

> ***Reflect:*** *If the people closest to you described your character to a stranger, what would they say? And is that the reputation you are intentionally building?*

Your legacy is not one dramatic moment. It is the accumulation of ordinary moments, lived with intention. Begin building it today.

CHAPTER 6

Crafting an Authentic Personal Brand

Here is the honest truth about personal branding: most of it is performance. And people can feel the difference.

A personal brand built on image rather than substance is a house of cards. It might look impressive for a while. But the first real test — the first crisis, the first honest conversation, the first time someone looks closely — reveals the gap between the performance and the person.

Authentic branding is simpler than we make it. It is just being, consistently, who you actually are.

Start with Values, Not Visuals

Before you think about how to present yourself, think about what you actually stand for. Write it down. Be specific. Not *I value integrity*, but *Here is what integrity looks like in my day-to-day decisions*. Not *I believe in people*, but *Here is how I actually show up for the people in my life*.

Your brand is what remains when the packaging is stripped away. Make sure it is built on something real.

Vulnerability Is Not Weakness — It Is Credibility

Michelle Obama's personal brand is among the most powerful in the world — and a significant part of its power comes from the fact that she talks about struggle. She talks about insecurity. She does not pretend she arrived fully formed. The result is that people believe her when she talks about strength, because they have watched her earn it.

Richard Branson's brand is built on risk-taking and adventure — but also on transparency about failure. He has talked openly about businesses that did not work, decisions he regrets, moments of uncertainty. That honesty is not a weakness in his brand. It is the reason people trust it.

Your story — including the hard parts — is your most valuable asset. Do not edit out the struggle. It is the part that makes the rest believable.

> ***Reflect:*** *If you could not describe yourself with any job title or credential, who would you be? What would remain?*

Building an authentic personal brand is really just the work of becoming — and staying — yourself. Everything else follows.

CHAPTER 7

Strategic Honesty: The Cornerstone of Leadership

When I use the phrase strategic honesty, I do not mean calculated deception wrapped in polite language. I mean something deeper and more demanding: the practice of telling the truth in a way that is timed, targeted, and genuinely helpful.

There is a difference between being honest and being honest well. Anyone can blurt out every thought they have. That is not courage — it is noise. Strategic honesty requires you to know what is true, to have the courage to say it, and to have the wisdom to say it in a way that actually serves the person you are talking to.

Transparency Creates the Conditions for Trust

Early in my leadership journey, I managed a district of twenty-six area directors. One of the things I noticed quickly was that people did not just want information — they wanted to feel included in the direction. So I communicated obsessively. Newsletters, social media, personal emails, all-hands meetings, one-on-ones. I made sure no one could say they did not know what we were trying to build together.

That transparency did not just keep people informed. It kept people committed. When people understand why, they show up differently than when they are simply told what.

Emotional Intelligence Is Not Optional

Leaders who are emotionally unaware — who cannot read a room, who cannot regulate their own reactions, who are oblivious to how their moods affect their teams — cause more damage than they realize. The emotional tone of a leader ripples outward constantly, for better or worse.

When I was under pressure during investigations and accusations at Toastmasters, I had to work very hard to manage what I was carrying internally so that it did not leak into how I treated my team. That was not about suppressing emotion — it was about not burdening others with what was mine to carry.

That discipline — choosing how to show up regardless of what you are feeling inside — is one of the hardest forms of leadership. And one of the most important.

> ***Reflect:*** *Think of a recent moment when you withheld an honest observation because you were afraid of how it would land. What would strategic honesty have looked like in that moment?*

Honesty is not a value you hold. It is a practice you return to, again and again, especially when it is hard.

CHAPTER 8

Character and Integrity Amidst Adversity

There is a story I have not often told publicly, because it touches something raw. But I believe in it too deeply to keep it out of this book.

When I was District Director of Toastmasters International, District 106, I was accused in writing of mistreating a female team member. The accusation made its way to World Headquarters. A formal investigation was launched. There was even a vote to remove me from my position.

I had done nothing wrong. I had followed every rule in the book. I had not selected this individual for a leadership role because credible reports from club members described a pattern of behavior — soliciting money and mistreating members — that made her unsuitable for the position. When I raised those concerns with her directly, she interpreted it as a personal attack and filed the complaint.

The investigation team reviewed everything. The case was dismissed. She eventually disappeared from the organization. And our district went on to win the President's Distinguished District award from World Headquarters — one of the highest honors in the organization.

But the months between the accusation and the dismissal were among the hardest of my leadership life.

What Adversity Reveals

I say all of this not to cast blame on anyone, but to name something important: adversity does not build character. It reveals it.

The character I had built over decades — through early struggles, through the refusal to take sides in disputes, through seven years of staying honest when it cost me — that character was the only thing standing between me and collapse when the false accusation arrived.

I knew who I was. The investigation team eventually knew it too. And the members of my district knew it long before the investigation began.

Mahatma Gandhi's commitment to nonviolence was tested — not hypothetically, but in prison, in the face of real violence, in moments when retaliation would have been understandable. His integrity was not a badge he wore in easy times. It was a practice he maintained in impossible ones.

That is what I mean by character amidst adversity.

> **Reflect:** Is there a current challenge in your life that is testing your character? What is it revealing about you — and are you willing to let that information shape you?

Character is not built in the boardroom or the classroom. It is built in the moments when everything is falling apart and you still choose to be exactly who you said you were.

CHAPTER 9
Unlocking the Power of Truth and Transparency

I want to tell you about the time I stole five thousand dollars.

I was in college, working as a cashier to help pay for my education. One day, I noticed a surplus in the cash register — five thousand dollars that should not have been there. I looked carefully at the accounts. There was no explanation for it.

And I needed money badly. Tuition was due. I was exhausted. The temptation was real.

I took the money. Then, for a week, I could not sleep. My conscience would not let me rest. Finally, I went to the owner and confessed everything — told him I had taken it, told him I had been wrong, offered to have it deducted from my salary over time.

He smiled.

He told me the money had been placed there intentionally. It was a test of integrity. He had known what I did within hours. He had been watching how long it would take me to come to him.

From that day forward, he trusted me completely. Never again did he check my work or question my accounts.

The Weight of Hidden Truth

Dishonesty is exhausting. People do not always calculate this cost when they choose to conceal something. But the energy required to maintain a lie — to remember what you said, to whom, and in what version — is enormous. Worse, it corrodes your relationship with yourself.

Truth is lighter. Not always easier, but always lighter.

Navigating the Hard Conversations

Later in my career, I found myself in another situation involving financial records — two managers in a dispute, both claiming the other had misrepresented the accounts. I was the administrative assistant. I knew the truth.

Both men were senior to me. Both were more powerful. And both, in different ways, wanted me to confirm their version of events.

I shared the accurate financial statements. I said clearly that decisions needed to be based on facts, not on power struggles. I did not choose sides. I just chose truth.

The tools from Kerry Patterson and colleagues in Crucial Conversations helped me develop the skill of staying composed while saying difficult things. That book — and the practice it describes — has stayed with me ever since.

> **Reflect:** *Is there a truth you have been holding back — with a colleague, a family member, or yourself? What would become possible if you said it?*

Transparency does not mean sharing every thought you have. It means not hiding what matters. It means building relationships on a foundation that can actually hold weight.

CHAPTER 10
Innovative Solutions Through Honesty

The most creative conversations I have ever been part of started with someone saying: I do not know.

That might seem like a strange thing to say in a chapter about innovation. But think about it. When everyone in a room is pretending to know more than they do, the energy goes into protecting positions. When someone is honest about uncertainty, the energy goes into solving the problem.

Honesty creates space for creativity. Pretense closes it.

Admitting Limitation as a Leadership Strength

I made it a habit, throughout my career, to acknowledge what I did not know. Not performatively — not as a rhetorical strategy — but genuinely. When I said that out loud, it gave other people permission to offer what they did have.

The result was not a diminished team. It was a more honest one. And honest teams, in my experience, solve problems faster and more creatively than ones where everyone is performing expertise.

Leading a Team Through Transformation

When I led the shift from waterfall to agile development — a change that many on my team had initially resisted — one of the things that made the difference was radical transparency about what we were trying to accomplish and how we were doing.

Every retrospective was honest. We celebrated what had worked. We named what had not. We shared our metrics openly, including the unflattering ones. And because people could see the real picture, they could engage with the real problems. Improvement followed from that engagement — not from me having all the answers, but from all of us being willing to look clearly at the truth.

SpaceX's commitment to publicly sharing the results of failed launches — not just the successes — is one of the reasons it moved faster than anyone expected. When you are honest about failure, you learn from it faster.

> ***Reflect:*** *In your current work or home life, where are you performing certainty you do not have? What would it cost — and what might it gain — to be honest about that?*

Honesty is not just an ethical value. It is a practical tool. Teams that tell each other the truth outperform teams that do not. It is that straightforward.

PART II

Core Principles of Integrity-Centered Leadership

The inner work of Part I prepares you for the outer work of Part II. Here we move from foundation to practice — the daily disciplines that build trust, reputation, and the kind of influence that lasts.

CHAPTER 11

Humility: A Pathway to Leadership Excellence

I want to tell you about a community meeting I attended years ago. The group was discussing the purchase of a property for a cultural center — an exciting project, full of possibility. But as I listened, it became clear that the conversation had skipped past a fundamental question: how exactly would they acquire the property? There was talk of fundraising. Of renovations. Of what the center might look like once it was built. But no one was asking about the actual purchase.

I raised my hand. I asked some direct questions about the financial realities. The committee was not pleased. They deflected. Someone made a joke at my expense. I left the meeting feeling foolish, wondering if I should have stayed quiet.

Two weeks later, they invited me back — and offered me a leadership role.

They had heard me. They had just needed time to recognize that what I was saying was useful, even if it had been uncomfortable.

The Difference Between Confidence and Arrogance

Humility is not the absence of confidence. It is the willingness to hold confidence lightly enough to remain teachable.

When leaders mistake arrogance for confidence, they stop learning — and the moment they stop learning, they stop listening. They convince themselves they already know. That false certainty is one of the most dangerous forms of leadership failure.

I have three master's degrees. I still take courses. Not because I have to, but because the world keeps changing and I want to stay useful in it.

Servant Leadership in Practice

Simon Sinek describes the best leaders as the ones who create a circle of safety around their teams — who put others first, who absorb difficulty rather than passing it down. That image has stayed with me.

When I was leading the district, my job was not to be impressive. It was to make my team effective. Every coaching conversation, every piece of guidance I offered, every resource I connected someone with — it was all in service of helping them do their job well. My success was their success. That is not a philosophy. It is a practice.

> ***Reflect:*** *Where in your leadership do you prioritize being right over being open? What would change if you led from curiosity instead of certainty?*

The most effective leaders I have ever known were genuinely surprised by what they did not know. That surprise kept them sharp, kept them humble, and kept them growing.

CHAPTER 12

Work Ethics: The Bridge from Poverty to Prosperity

When I was struggling to pay for college, I worked at a grocery store. One day, my boss pulled me aside and told me he wanted me to sell a product that was counterfeit — designed to look like the real thing but substantially inferior. He made it clear there was good money in it.

I was a parent of two young sons. I was barely making ends meet. The temptation was real.

I declined. I told him, as respectfully as I could, that I could not do it — that my sons were watching me, and that I did not want the example I set for them to be one built on deception. He was irritated at first. Then he nodded. He told me later that he respected the answer.

A decade later, I wrote this chapter with my sons in mind, and they are both thriving. Not because I provided everything for them. Because I tried, as consistently as I could, to model what I actually believed.

Why Work Ethic Is More Than Working Hard

Work ethic is not about logging the most hours. It is about approaching your responsibilities with honesty, consistency, and a genuine desire to add value rather than just collect a paycheck.

The supervisor who once blocked my promotions — who created friction for me at every turn — ended up writing me one of the finest professional recommendations I have ever received. He told the hiring panel that he had never been able to question my integrity, only my usefulness to him. Coming from the man who had worked against me for years, that was the most honest evaluation he could offer.

That is what consistent work ethic builds over time. A record that speaks for you even when your advocates are not in the room.

Reflect: *If you were no longer in your current role tomorrow, what would your colleagues say about how you worked? And is that the legacy you want to leave?*

Work ethic is not built in the spotlight. It is built in the thousand small moments when you choose quality over convenience, honesty over ease, and service over recognition.

CHAPTER 13

Transforming Challenges into Opportunities

Every obstacle has two faces. One is the face it shows you immediately — the disruption, the fear, the cost. The other face takes longer to see. It is the question: what might this make possible?

I have spent most of my life learning to look for the second face.

Healthy Conflict as a Creative Force

Teams that never disagree do not produce their best work. Agreement feels comfortable, but it is often just the absence of honesty. When people care about each other enough to challenge each other — when they trust each other enough to say what they actually think — that is when the best ideas emerge.

Patrick Lencioni's work on team dynamics is useful here. He shows that the inability to tolerate productive conflict is one of the core dysfunctions of teams. The cure is trust — and trust, as we have seen throughout this book, is built through honesty.

Apple, SpaceX, and the Companies That Failed Forward

Steve Jobs returned to Apple after being pushed out of the company he founded. The humiliation of that departure became the furnace in which his best leadership qualities were forged. He came back different. More focused. More willing to listen. More clear about what he believed.

SpaceX launched rockets that exploded. Publicly. On video. And then they launched them again, incorporating what they had learned. That willingness to fail visibly — and to treat each failure as data — is one of the defining characteristics of companies that eventually change the world.

Reflect: What challenge in your life right now could become an opportunity — if you changed the lens through which you are looking at it?

Challenges are not detours from the journey. They are the journey. The only question is whether you will move through them or be stopped by them.

CHAPTER 14

Accountability and Growth through Mistakes

I want to tell you about my attempt to break into software engineering.

I studied. I trained. I practiced. And I went on interview after interview, failing most of them. The technical questions were difficult — I understood the concepts, but translating that understanding into quick, confident answers under pressure was something I struggled with.

After a particularly discouraging stretch, I changed my approach. Instead of studying more, I started studying the interviews themselves. I wrote down the questions that stumped me. I practiced explaining the logic behind my thinking rather than rushing to the final answer.

The interviewers started responding differently. They were interested not in whether I could produce perfect code on demand, but in how I thought through problems. When I showed them the process — even the parts where I was uncertain — they trusted me more, not less.

That experience taught me more about accountability than any book I have read. Because the first step was admitting, honestly, that my previous approach was not working.

The Cleansing Power of Ownership

There is something almost physically relieving about saying: I made a mistake, and I take responsibility for it. Not the defensive quasi-apology that really means I am sorry you feel that way. But the full, clean admission: I was wrong, and here is what I am going to do about it.

NASA, in the aftermath of the Challenger disaster, did not look away from what had gone wrong. They opened it all up — the engineering failures, the communication failures, the cultural failures that had allowed warning signs to be ignored. And from that painful transparency came genuine safety improvements that have protected astronauts ever since.

That is what honest accountability makes possible. Not just individual growth, but systemic improvement.

> ***Reflect:*** *Is there a mistake you are still carrying without fully owning it? What would it feel like to put it down — completely — by acknowledging it and making it right?*

No one becomes a better leader by being perfect. Everyone becomes a better leader by learning to recover from imperfection with honesty and grace.

CHAPTER 15

Integrity in Personal Brand Building

When I was eight years old, I had a toy I loved — nothing fancy, but mine. One day, someone offered me a shiny new thing in exchange for it. I remember the pull of it, that bright distraction. I also remember holding onto what was mine.

That small childhood moment has stayed with me as a kind of metaphor for the temptations that come in building a reputation. There will always be something shiny — a shortcut, an exaggeration, a small deception that seems harmless in the moment. And there will always be a cost when you reach for it.

The Difference Between Image and Brand

Image is what you project. Brand is what you have earned.

Patagonia has earned its brand. The company's environmental commitments are not marketing campaigns — they are operational realities, backed by decades of consistent choices. Oprah Winfrey has earned her brand. The authenticity that audiences feel when they watch her is the result of years of honest self-expression, including the uncomfortable parts.

You earn your brand the same way — not by managing perception, but by living consistently with your values even when no one is applauding.

> *Reflect:* If someone followed you for a week without telling you, what personal brand would they observe? And does that brand reflect who you actually want to be?

Your brand is not built on your best days. It is built on your most ordinary ones — when no one is watching, when it is inconvenient, when the shortcut would have been so easy.

CHAPTER 16
From Foe to Friend: Turning Adversaries into Allies

The investigation panel that was formed to review the accusations against me as District Director became, in time, some of my strongest allies. The person who had accused me eventually left. The people who had scrutinized my record most carefully were the ones who came away most convinced of my character.

I did not engineer that. I just stayed who I was.

That experience confirmed something I have believed for a long time: the best way to turn an adversary into an ally is not strategy. It is consistency. Show up the same way under scrutiny that you do when things are easy. Give people enough time and enough evidence to see who you actually are.

Empathy as a Leadership Skill

Brené Brown's research on leadership and vulnerability makes a point I have seen confirmed in real life: when leaders are willing to acknowledge their own imperfections — when they are willing to sit in discomfort rather than defend against it — they create the conditions in which others can do the same.

The people who were initially against me could feel that I was not performing. I was not managing impressions. I was simply leading. And leading from that authentic place, over time, created enough safety for even skeptical people to soften.

The Arbinger Principle: Getting Out of the Box

The Arbinger Institute writes about what they call being in the box — a state in which you see other people as obstacles rather than as full human beings. When you are in the box, every interaction is about defending your position. When you get out of it, you can actually see the person in front of you.

I try to stay out of the box, especially with people who challenge me. It does not always come naturally. But it is always worth the effort.

> **Reflect:** Think of someone in your life you have been treating as an adversary. What might they need that you have not yet considered? What might change if you led with that understanding?

The people who push back hardest are often the ones who care most. Treat them accordingly.

PART III

Advanced Concepts in Integrity-Centered Leadership

Part III moves into the harder terrain — where the right answer is not obvious, where pressure tests principles, and where staying true to your values requires more than good intentions. These chapters are for leaders who are ready to go deeper.

CHAPTER 17

Authenticity Over False Branding

In an age when everyone is curating their story — trimming the rough edges, amplifying the highlights, performing a version of themselves that is slightly more confident and significantly more polished — authenticity has become an increasingly rare and valuable thing.

People can feel it when it is missing.

What Inauthenticity Actually Costs

False branding has a tax that is rarely calculated upfront. The energy required to maintain a persona that does not match your reality is enormous. You have to remember what you said, and to whom, and in which version. You have to manage the gap between the performance and the person. Over time, that gap becomes a source of chronic low-grade stress.

And eventually — often at the worst possible moment — it collapses.

Enron's collapse was, at its root, a failure of authenticity. The company projected an image of health and innovation that had no relationship to its actual financial reality. When the truth came out, it was catastrophic — not just for the company, but for thousands of employees, shareholders, and families.

Dove, Airbnb, and the Power of Genuine Representation

Dove's Campaign for Real Beauty succeeded not because it was clever marketing, but because it was honest. It acknowledged something that every woman knew to be true — that beauty standards had been manufactured, not discovered — and it said so plainly. People responded because they felt seen.

Airbnb was built on the idea that strangers could trust each other enough to share their homes. That model only works if the trust is real — if what you see when you book is actually what you get. Every policy, every review system, every design choice in the platform is oriented around making authenticity practical.

Reflect: *Where in your professional or personal life are you projecting something that does not match your reality? What would it cost to close that gap?*

The performance of authenticity is not authenticity. You cannot fake it sustainably. The path forward is always the same: become who you are saying you are.

CHAPTER 18

Sustainable Success: Rejecting Get-Rich-Quick Thinking

There is no shortcut worth taking. I know that sounds like something a grandmother would cross-stitch on a pillow — and maybe she would be right. But I want to say it plainly, because the culture we live in tells us constantly that there is a faster way, an easier path, a method someone has discovered that allows success without the work.

There isn't. Not the lasting kind.

The Illusion of Instant Gratification

Short-term gains can look a great deal like success, especially from a distance. The problem is that they are often borrowed against the future. The person who takes a shortcut may get ahead temporarily, but they also absorb a kind of invisible debt — in credibility, in character, in the trust of others who were watching.

Warren Buffett has spent decades making the same point in different ways: the best investments are the boring ones, held long enough for the compounding to do its work. That principle applies not just to money, but to reputation, relationships, and leadership.

Delayed Gratification as a Practice

I did not achieve anything significant quickly. I was a site clerk before I was a finance director. I was a finance director before I became a technology leader. I earned each degree while working full time, while raising sons, while serving my community.

That slowness was not failure. It was preparation.

The person I became by doing things the long way was far more capable — and far more trustworthy — than the person I would have been had I found a shortcut. The work itself changes you. That is the part the shortcut cuts out.

Mahatma Gandhi's commitment to nonviolence was not just a tactical decision — it was a years-long practice of choosing principle over expediency, again and again, until that practice became unshakeable. The results did not come quickly. But they lasted.

> **Reflect:** *Where in your life are you choosing the fast path over the right one? What is it costing you that you might not be counting?*

The richest life — in every sense of that word — is built slowly, deliberately, and honestly. There is no version of sustainable success that skips that work.

CHAPTER 19

Wealth Through Purpose and Fulfillment

I have known people who had everything money could buy and felt they had nothing. I have known people who had very little money and felt deeply wealthy. The difference, in every case, was purpose.

When I was still a young man in Nepal, my purpose was simple and urgent: provide for my family, create opportunities my siblings did not have. That purpose made the work meaningful, even when the work was hard.

As I moved through different phases of life, the purpose evolved. But it never disappeared. It has always been the engine underneath whatever I was doing.

Daniel Pink and the Anatomy of Motivation

Daniel Pink's research on motivation identifies three core drivers: autonomy, mastery, and purpose. Money activates behavior on the surface. Purpose activates it at the root.

Leaders who communicate purpose — who give their teams a clear sense of why the work matters beyond the paycheck — create engaged people. Leaders who treat work purely transactionally create people who show up but are not really there.

Simon Sinek's Start with Why makes the same point from a different angle: great leaders and great organizations begin with a clear sense of purpose and build everything else from there. The why shapes the what. Purpose shapes action.

Contributing to Others' Well-Being

One of the most reliable paths to personal fulfillment I have discovered is contribution. When I serve at a district level, managing thousands of volunteers who are themselves learning to lead — I am not thinking about compensation. I am thinking about the person in front of me who came to this organization with a dream of becoming a better communicator, a better leader, a better version of themselves.

Helping that person move forward a little faster, feel a little less alone in the journey — that is wealth. Not the kind that shows up on a balance sheet. The kind that makes you feel, at the end of the day, that your presence in the world actually mattered.

> ***Reflect:*** *What is the purpose underneath your work? Not the job description — the actual reason that gets you out of bed? If you cannot answer that clearly, it may be worth sitting with the question.*

True prosperity is not a destination. It is a by-product of purpose-driven living, built day by day through meaningful work, genuine contribution, and an honest relationship with what actually matters to you.

CHAPTER 20

Transforming Failure into Positive Change

Thomas Edison is said to have described his failed attempts to invent the lightbulb as having discovered ten thousand ways that would not work. Whether the quote is exactly accurate matters less than the spirit of it: the man failed, repeatedly, and treated each failure as information rather than verdict.

That relationship with failure — treating it as data rather than shame — is one of the most important things I know about success.

Failure Is a Teacher, Not a Verdict

There was a period in my career when I was trying to break into software engineering, and things were not going well. I went on interview after interview and came away without offers. The rational response might have been to conclude that the field was not for me.

But I had a different question: not Am I capable of this? but What am I missing? That question led me to study the interviews differently — to focus on articulating my reasoning process rather than rushing to answers. When I made that shift, the results changed.

The failure was not a verdict on my capability. It was an invitation to adjust.

SpaceX and the Public Failure Culture

SpaceX live-streamed failed rocket launches. They posted updates about what went wrong. They did not hide from failure — they published it.

There is something radical in that, and something instructive. When you are transparent about failure, you cannot be defined by it. You become, instead, the company — or the person — who is honest about the messy reality of doing difficult things and who keeps going anyway.

> *Reflect:* What failure from your recent past have you been treating as a verdict rather than a lesson? What information might that experience have been trying to give you?

The only failure that cannot be recovered from is the failure to learn. Everything else is curriculum.

CHAPTER 21

Making Informed Decisions Through Clarity

Good decisions come from clear thinking. Clear thinking comes from honest information. Honest information comes from people who trust that telling you the truth will not cost them.

That chain — from trust to truth to clarity to good decisions — is why everything else in this book matters when it comes to decision-making. You cannot make good decisions in an environment where people are afraid to tell you what they actually know.

The Role of Emotional Balance

Emotions are not the enemy of good decisions. Emotions that are unregulated — that flood the decision-making space without awareness or discipline — are the enemy.

I have made some of my worst decisions when I was reactive. When someone challenged me and I responded before I had thought clearly. When I was under pressure and grabbed the nearest available answer rather than the right one.

I have made my best decisions when I took time to let the emotional heat cool before committing to a course of action. That discipline — creating space between stimulus and response — is one of Viktor Frankl's great contributions to human understanding, and it applies directly to leadership.

Intuition and Analysis: Both Have a Place

There is a tendency in professional settings to treat data as superior to instinct. I understand why — data is shareable, justifiable, defensible in a meeting. Instinct is harder to explain.

But instinct, when it is developed through years of genuine experience, is its own form of data — pattern recognition operating below the level of conscious thought. The most effective decision-makers I know use both: they gather the facts, and they also listen to the feeling that arises when they sit with those facts.

Jacinda Ardern's leadership during the Christchurch attacks was notable precisely because she combined analytical clarity with emotional intelligence — she responded to the data of the situation while also responding to its human weight. Neither alone would have been sufficient.

> **Reflect:** *Think of a significant decision you are currently facing. What does the data say? What does your gut say? And where are those two things in tension?*

Clarity is not the absence of complexity. It is the capacity to see through complexity to what actually matters. Honesty, emotional balance, and willingness to stay in the question together create that capacity.

CHAPTER 22

Cultivating Self-Honesty and Growth

The hardest person to be honest with is yourself.

Other people, you can manage. You can shape what they see, emphasize what reflects well on you, minimize what does not. With yourself, eventually, the accounting comes due. You cannot hide from your own experience indefinitely.

Self-honesty is the practice of looking at that experience clearly — without flinching, without flattery, without the comfortable narrative that keeps you from growing.

The Mirror We Avoid

The Arbinger Institute's work on self-deception describes the way we construct elaborate justifications for our behavior — especially our worst behavior. We explain to ourselves why the thing we just did that we know was wrong was actually reasonable given the circumstances. We protect our self-image at the expense of our growth.

Getting out of that trap requires a specific kind of honesty — not self-flagellation, but clear seeing. What actually happened? What did I actually feel, and why? What did I actually do, and what did it accomplish?

Those questions, sat with honestly over time, are the engine of real self-development.

Self-Awareness as a Lifelong Practice

I am a different person than I was twenty years ago. I hope to be a different person in twenty more years — not unrecognizably different, but grown. The thing that creates that growth is not willpower or ambition. It is the consistent practice of asking: who am I actually being right now, and is that the person I want to be?

> *Reflect:* If you were to be genuinely honest with yourself about one pattern in your life that is holding you back — what would it be?

Self-honesty is not punishment. It is the most generous thing you can offer yourself — the opportunity to actually change, rather than continuing to act as if you already have.

CHAPTER 23

Avoiding Self-Sabotage Through Integrity

There is a particular kind of pain in recognizing that you have been your own worst obstacle. That the thing standing between you and the life you want has, in certain important ways, been you.

I have been there. Most of us have, if we are honest.

Self-sabotage rarely announces itself plainly. It disguises itself as prudence, as waiting for the right moment, as protecting yourself from failure by never quite trying. It looks like procrastination, like self-doubt repeated until it becomes belief, like fear of success dressed up as fear of failure.

The Box of Self-Deception

The Arbinger Institute calls it being in the box. When you are in the box, you see yourself as the hero of every story and everyone around you as either obstacle or supporting cast. You are right. They are wrong. Your behavior is justified. Theirs is not.

The problem with the box is that it seals you off from growth. You cannot learn from interactions you have already pre-interpreted. You cannot improve in relationships where you are always the innocent party.

Getting out of the box requires the hardest thing in leadership: the willingness to be wrong about yourself.

Integrity as the Antidote

When you are living in alignment with your values — when your actions and your stated beliefs are consistent — you remove one of the primary sources of self-sabotage. The internal conflict that comes from acting against your own values creates a kind of psychological static that interferes with everything.

Nelson Mandela spent twenty-seven years in prison. He did not emerge bitter, though he had every reason to be. He emerged with his values intact and his vision clear. The integrity he had maintained through imprisonment was the same integrity that made him capable of leading a country through reconciliation.

Reflect: *Where in your life are you acting against your own values — and what is that costing you in energy, focus, and peace of mind?*

The most powerful thing you can do to get out of your own way is to close the gap between who you say you are and how you actually live. That gap is where self-sabotage lives.

CHAPTER 24

Integrity as a Spiritual Practice

I want to say something that might seem unusual in a leadership book: integrity, at its deepest level, is a spiritual practice.

I do not mean that in a narrowly religious sense. I mean it in the sense that integrity — when you really live it — connects you to something larger than yourself. It connects you to a set of values that feel, at their root, sacred. Worth protecting. Worth sacrificing for.

The people who have held to their integrity through the most extreme circumstances — Mandela, Gandhi, Frankl — describe it as something that gave them access to an inner source of strength that external circumstances could not touch. The body could be imprisoned. The inner life could not.

Mindful Leadership

Mindfulness in leadership means something simple but demanding: being fully present with the decision in front of you, rather than reacting from habit, fear, or past experience.

When I am in a difficult conversation, the practice is to notice what is happening inside me without being controlled by it. To feel the discomfort of disagreement without immediately trying to resolve it through defense or deflection. To stay with the truth, even when staying is uncomfortable.

That practice — again and again — over years, becomes something. It becomes who you are.

> **Reflect:** *What would it mean to treat your daily choices as a spiritual practice — as something that connects you to your deepest values and shapes who you are becoming?*

Integrity is not a policy. It is a practice. And like all practices, it grows stronger each time you choose it, especially when it is hard.

CHAPTER 25
Envisioning Your Future Self with Integrity

One of the most useful questions you can ask yourself is: who do I want to be in ten years? Not what do I want to achieve — but who do I want to be?

The distinction matters. Achievements can be granted or taken by circumstances. Character is built by you, through a long series of choices, over time. The person you become is the result of who you chose to be when the choices were small and the stakes were invisible.

Goal Setting as Identity Work

When I picture my future self, I am not imagining a title or a salary. I am imagining a person who is still learning, still generous with his knowledge, still honest in difficult conversations, still the same person at home that he is in public.

The goals I set are in service of that person — not the other way around. I do not pursue a goal because it will make me successful. I pursue it because it is consistent with the person I am trying to become.

That reframe changes everything about how you evaluate opportunities. Instead of asking Will this advance my career? you ask Is this consistent with who I want to be? Those two questions often lead to different answers.

Embracing Transformation Honestly

Change is uncomfortable, and growth often requires us to let go of a version of ourselves that felt safe or familiar. That letting go takes honesty — the willingness to admit that the current approach is not working, that the current path is not leading where you want to go.

It also takes courage. Not dramatic courage, but the small, daily courage of continuing to work toward something when the results are not yet visible.

> *Reflect:* Picture yourself ten years from now, having lived with integrity throughout. What does that person look like? How does she or he move through the world? What do the people around that person say about who they are?

The future self you are building is not a fantasy. It is the logical extension of the choices you are making today. Choose accordingly.

CHAPTER 26
Investing in Emotional Integrity and Trust

Trust is the most fragile and the most essential element of any relationship — personal or professional. It is built slowly, over many interactions, and can be damaged or destroyed by a single one.

Emotional integrity — the alignment between what you feel, what you say, and how you behave — is the foundation of trust. When people sense that you are performing an emotion rather than actually feeling it, they do not trust you. When they sense consistency between your inner life and your outer behavior, they do.

The Leader Who Cannot Hide

I have known leaders who believed they could compartmentalize their emotions completely — who thought they could be in a difficult personal situation and lead their teams as if nothing were happening. In my experience, that compartmentalization rarely works as well as the leader thinks it does.

Teams feel the emotional temperature of their leaders. They may not be able to name what is happening, but they sense it. When a leader is carrying unacknowledged fear or anger or grief into a team setting, it affects the environment whether the leader intends it to or not.

Emotional integrity does not mean sharing everything with your team. It means not pretending to feel what you do not feel, and not acting as if difficult realities are not real. It means being honest, at some level, about where you are — while still being able to lead.

Nelson Mandela's Emotional Leadership

What Mandela demonstrated after his release from prison was emotional integrity at scale. He did not pretend to feel reconciled when he was not. He did not perform forgiveness as a political strategy. He actually worked, deeply and publicly, toward the values he stated — and the South Africa that watched him do it trusted him because of it.

Brené Brown's research on vulnerability describes the same phenomenon: leaders who are willing to be genuinely open — not performatively vulnerable, but actually honest about their human experience — create the conditions in which others feel safe to be themselves.

> ***Reflect:*** *Where in your leadership are your stated emotions and your actual emotions out of alignment? What might change if you brought them closer together?*

The deepest trust is built not by being impressive, but by being real. Give people the gift of your genuine presence, and they will give you theirs in return.

PART IV

Integrity in Action

This final part is where everything becomes practice. The principles of Parts I through III meet the real world — the difficult relationships, the public-facing choices, the test of whether what you believe is actually how you live. This is where integrity either holds or it doesn't.

CHAPTER 27

Commitment to Your Path of Integrity

I have been on this path for a long time. And I will tell you honestly: there have been moments when I was tired. When it would have been so much easier to compromise, to take the side that powerful people were pressuring me to take, to give in to the version of events that was more convenient than true.

I did not take those exits. Not because I am exceptionally strong, but because I had, by that point in my life, made integrity so fundamental to my identity that departing from it would have meant becoming someone I could not recognize.

That is what long-term commitment to a value does. It stops being a choice you make every day and starts being something closer to who you are.

Resilience Is Not Toughness

People sometimes confuse resilience with toughness — the ability to feel nothing, to be unmoved, to power through. That is not resilience. Resilience is the capacity to be moved, to be affected, to feel the difficulty — and to keep going anyway.

Sherron Watkins, who blew the whistle on the Enron fraud, was not unaffected by what she did. She was deeply afraid. She felt isolated. She did it anyway, because her values required it of her.

That is resilience. Not the absence of fear, but the commitment to proceed despite it.

External Pressure Will Always Come

In every organization, in every community, there are forces that push you away from your values. The pressure to belong, to agree, to not make waves, to prioritize short-term peace over long-term truth.

The leaders who navigate that pressure most effectively are the ones who are most clear about who they are underneath the pressure. Clarity of identity is the best protection I know against external forces that would shape you in directions you do not want to go.

> ***Reflect:*** *What external pressures are currently testing your commitment to your values? And what would it look like to hold steady — not against those pressures, but through them?*

Commitment to integrity is not a one-time decision. It is a practice renewed every day, in the moments that test it. The strength to renew that practice comes from knowing — deeply, clearly — who you are and what you are committed to.

CHAPTER 28

Making Amends and Restoring Integrity

I have made mistakes as a leader. Real ones — not the small, forgettable kind, but the kind that affected people who trusted me, the kind that required me to sit with the discomfort of having fallen short of who I said I was.

Making amends is not comfortable. But it is also not optional if you care about the long-term health of your relationships and your character.

What a Real Apology Looks Like

There is a kind of apology that is really about reducing the discomfort of the apologizer — a quick statement designed to clear the air and move on. And then there is the kind of apology that is actually about the person who was harmed.

The second kind acknowledges what happened without minimization. It takes full responsibility without caveats. It asks what can be done to make things right, and then follows through. It does not expect to be forgiven quickly, or at all.

That kind of apology is rare and enormously powerful. It communicates to the person receiving it that their experience mattered, that you take them seriously, that you value the relationship more than your ego.

Nelson Mandela's Model

Mandela's commitment to forgiveness and reconciliation after twenty-seven years in prison is the most extraordinary example of making amends at scale that I know. He was not the one who needed to apologize — but he chose the path of healing over the path of retribution, because he understood that South Africa's future depended on it.

He did not do that because it was easy. He did it because it was right. And his willingness to lead from that place of hard-won generosity made him, arguably, the most credible leader of the twentieth century.

Reflect: *Is there someone in your life — a colleague, a family member, a friend — to whom you owe a real apology? What has been stopping you from offering it?*

Integrity, once damaged, can be restored. Not automatically, not quickly, but genuinely — through consistent action over time. The restoration of trust, when it comes, is one of the most meaningful things a leader can experience.

CHAPTER 29

Leveraging Credibility for Protection

I have already shared parts of the story of the false accusation I faced as District Director. What I want to focus on in this chapter is not the accusation itself, but what protected me from it.

It was credibility. Built over years, through thousands of small interactions. The people who served on the investigation panel knew my work. They had seen how I operated. When the accusation arrived, they did not dismiss it — they took it seriously and investigated thoroughly. And what they found, when they looked closely, was consistent with everything they had already observed.

Credibility is the kind of protection no one can manufacture in a crisis. You either built it beforehand, or you did not.

How a Strong Reputation Becomes a Shield

False accusations succeed most easily when the accused has a weak reputation — when there is no established record to contradict the claim. My record was clear. Not because I had planned to be falsely accused someday, but because I had simply been who I said I was, consistently, for long enough that people knew it.

That is the strange alchemy of credibility: you cannot build it in anticipation of needing it. You build it by not thinking about it — by just doing the right thing, over and over, because it is the right thing.

Communication as a Credibility Tool

One lesson I drew from that experience was about language and nuance. I write in English, which is my second language. In the investigation, some of my written communications to junior leaders were examined and I was advised to be more careful with my phrasing — to be conscious of how different word choices might land, especially on matters of gender and inclusion.

That was useful feedback, and I took it seriously. Leadership at scale requires not just good intentions but good execution — including the execution of written communication in a language that carries cultural nuance I am still learning.

> ***Reflect:*** *What is your current credibility account balance — with your team, your organization, your family? And are you making regular deposits?*

Credibility is not a static thing. It requires ongoing investment. But when the crisis comes — and it will come — it is worth everything.

CHAPTER 30
Utilizing Credibility for Positive Impact

Credibility without direction is wasted. Trust that does not serve any larger purpose is just social capital sitting in a vault.

The leaders I most admire have always understood this. They worked hard to earn credibility, and then they spent it — on causes that mattered, on people who needed advocacy, on directions that their teams might not have found courage to take without someone trustworthy leading the way.

The Ripple Effect of Earned Trust

When Abraham Lincoln made the most consequential decision of his presidency — to issue the Emancipation Proclamation in the midst of a war — he was drawing on credibility. He had earned the trust of enough people through years of consistent, honest, principled leadership that they were willing to follow him into profoundly uncertain territory.

That is the power of credibility in motion. It does not just protect you. It propels others.

Leading by Example at Every Level

You do not have to be a president or a district director to use your credibility for impact. Every person who holds the trust of others has the opportunity to use that trust to lift someone else.

The parent who models honesty for a child. The manager who advocates for a team member who cannot advocate for themselves. The colleague who speaks up in a meeting when everyone else has gone quiet. These are acts of credibility in action, and they matter enormously in the lives they touch.

> *Reflect:* What cause, person, or idea is worth spending your credibility on right now? And what has been stopping you?

Credibility is not meant to be hoarded. It is meant to be invested. The return on that investment — in the lives you touch and the changes you help create — is the closest thing to legacy that most of us will ever build.

CHAPTER 31

Treating Others Well: The Ethical Imperative

Simon Sinek says it simply: Leadership is not about being in charge. It is about taking care of those in your charge.

I believe that completely. And I believe it extends beyond formal leadership roles to every relationship in our lives.

The way you treat the people who can do nothing for you — the administrative assistant, the janitor, the most junior member of the team — reveals more about your character than how you treat the people who hold power over you. Character is not what you perform under observation. It is what you do in the small, unscripted moments.

The Golden Rule Under Pressure

It is easy to treat people well when things are going smoothly. The test of ethical behavior is always whether it holds under pressure — when you are tired, when you are frustrated, when someone has disappointed you or pushed back against you in a way that triggered your defensiveness.

I have not always passed that test. There have been moments in my leadership — especially under the stress of investigations and organizational conflict — when I was shorter with people than I should have been, when I held the weight of my situation in ways that leaked into interactions I wish I could redo.

What I know now is that those moments are not failures to be hidden. They are data — invitations to pay closer attention to where I need to grow.

Empathy as a Structural Practice

Empathy is not a personality trait. It is a practice — a deliberate act of asking, genuinely, what it is like to be the person in front of you right now.

Brené Brown's work on leadership makes this point compellingly: the leaders who create the healthiest environments are the ones who make empathy structural — who build it into how meetings are run, how feedback is given, how conflicts are addressed. They do not leave it to personality or good days. They build it into the system.

Reflect: *Think of the person in your life you find most difficult to treat with consistent kindness and respect. What do you think their experience is? And what would change if you approached them from that understanding?*

Leadership is, at its deepest level, an act of care. Not soft care — rigorous, honest, demanding care that tells people the truth and holds them to high standards while never forgetting their humanity.

CHAPTER 32

Safeguarding Your Unshakeable Integrity

By now, you have read about integrity in nearly every context I know to apply it. Under accusation. Under financial temptation. Under the pressure of powerful people who wanted something from me. In the small, everyday moments that no one watches.

I want to spend this chapter on the practice of protecting your integrity — not defensively, but proactively. Because integrity, like any important thing, requires active stewardship.

Self-Reflection as Maintenance

The people who maintain their integrity over decades tend to have a practice of regular self-examination. They ask themselves, honestly and often: Am I still who I say I am? Are there gaps between my stated values and my actual behavior that I have been ignoring?

That practice is not comfortable. But it is essential. The gaps that are caught early are much easier to close than the ones that are allowed to widen over years.

The Danger of Slow Drift

Integrity rarely collapses dramatically. It tends to erode slowly — through small compromises that each seem reasonable in isolation. A slight exaggeration here. A small deception of omission there. A gradual drift in the standards you hold yourself to.

The Enron executives did not arrive at massive fraud overnight. They got there through years of small rationalizations, each building on the last. Staying clear of those extremes requires the maintenance practices that this chapter is about. Regular self-reflection. Accountability relationships with people who will tell you the truth. Clear ethical boundaries established before you are tested by them.

> *Reflect:* When did you last take stock of your own integrity — honestly, specifically, without flattering yourself? What did you find?

Your integrity is your most valuable asset. Treat it accordingly. Guard it. Examine it regularly. And when you find it needs repair, repair it immediately, before the damage compounds.

CHAPTER 33

Honoring Commitments and Building Trust

I want to tell you about the first piece of land I ever bought.

I was nineteen years old. I had just finished high school. I was dealing with people who were older, more experienced, and significantly more educated than me. We completed the transaction, but there was something that troubled me afterward: there had been no formal paperwork. No receipt. No legal documentation that I could hold.

I asked my relatives how I could be sure the sale was real.

They told me: the man I bought from is a man of his word. He will show up.

He did show up. Even when his sons criticized him for selling the land at a lower price than he could have gotten. He faced that pressure and honored his commitment anyway, because he was someone whose word meant something.

I made a decision that day: I wanted to be that person.

The Compound Interest of Kept Promises

Trust is built through the accumulation of kept commitments. Not dramatic ones — though those matter too — but the ordinary ones. Showing up to the meeting you said you would attend. Delivering the report when you said you would. Returning the phone call.

Each kept commitment adds a small deposit to the trust account. Each broken one makes a withdrawal. The account that matters most in your life is not the financial one. It is the trust one.

Simon Sinek's Circle of Safety

Sinek writes that effective leaders act as a circle of safety for their teams — they put the well-being of the people around them first, they absorb difficulty rather than passing it down, they honor their commitments to their people even when it costs them something personally.

I tried to practice that throughout my years in leadership. I did not always succeed. But the intention was clear: the people who followed me should be able to trust that I meant what I said.

> ***Reflect:*** *Where in your life have you made a commitment — to yourself or to someone else — that you have been slowly letting slide? What would it mean to renew that commitment today?*

Your word is your bond. In every domain of your life, in every relationship, the question of whether people can count on you is one of the most important things about you. Build a record they can believe.

CHAPTER 34

Presenting Yourself as a Trustworthy Leader

There is an important difference between self-promotion and self-revelation.

Self-promotion is about managing perception. Self-revelation is about telling the truth about who you are, what you stand for, and what you can genuinely offer. The first is exhausting and ultimately fragile. The second is the basis of real trust.

Consistency as the Core of Credibility

The leaders I trust most are not necessarily the most impressive or the most charismatic. They are the ones I can predict — not because they are boring, but because they are consistent. I know who they will be tomorrow. I know how they will handle a difficult situation. I know that what they say privately is what they say publicly.

That consistency is not an accident. It is the result of someone who has done the inner work — who knows what they value and has aligned their behavior with those values over a long enough period that the alignment has become second nature.

Balancing Confidence with Openness

Confidence in your abilities and openness to being wrong are not opposites. The best leaders I know are genuinely confident and genuinely curious. They know what they are good at. They also know the limits of their own perspective and actively seek information they might be missing.

That combination — confident enough to lead, humble enough to learn — is what people follow. Not because it is an impressive performance, but because it is trustworthy. You know the person is not going to pretend to know things they do not know, and that matters enormously when the decisions are hard.

> *Reflect:* How would you describe yourself to someone who has never met you? And how closely does that description match how the people closest to you would describe you?

The most powerful personal brand you can build is the truth of who you are, lived consistently over time. That is not a marketing strategy. It is a character strategy. And it is the only one that actually works.

CHAPTER 35

Unlimited Credibility: A Continuous Pursuit

Credibility is not a destination. You do not arrive, collect the certificate, and stop working. It is a living thing that requires ongoing care, ongoing consistency, and ongoing honesty about where it has been damaged and needs repair.

The most credible people I know are the most humble about their credibility. They do not rest on their record. They treat each interaction as a new opportunity to either add to or subtract from the account.

Setbacks Are Part of the Journey

Everyone who has built genuine credibility has also, at some point, damaged it and had to rebuild. The rebuilding process — honest, patient, demonstrated through action rather than declaration — is itself a form of credibility building.

The Enron scandal is instructive precisely because it shows what happens when credibility is performed rather than built. The company was celebrated for years. The credibility was not real. When the reality became clear, there was nothing underneath to hold.

The whistleblowers of the world — Sherron Watkins, Malala Yousafzai in her own very different context — demonstrate the opposite. People who held to their values under pressure, whose credibility was not a performance but a practice, and whose sustained integrity eventually changed what was possible.

> *Reflect:* If you imagine yourself at the end of your career, looking back — what would you most want the record to show? And are the choices you are making today consistent with building that record?

Unlimited credibility is not about having no blemishes. It is about an orientation toward growth, honesty, and repair — a commitment to keep working on who you are, for as long as you have the opportunity to do so.

CHAPTER 36

Failure as a Steppingstone to Achievement

Winston Churchill said: Success is not final, failure is not fatal. It is the courage to continue that counts.

I have lived that quote many times — in career shifts that did not go as planned, in leadership decisions that missed the mark, in personal moments where I fell short of the person I wanted to be.

Each time, the question was not whether to recover. The question was how honestly to learn.

From Failure to Data

SpaceX's iterative design approach — launching, failing, studying the wreckage, improving, launching again — is one of the most visible examples of treating failure as data in modern business. The company did not celebrate failure for its own sake. It celebrated the learning that failure enabled.

Google's internal culture of encouraging employees to take on projects that might fail — sometimes explicitly called fail forward — reflects the same principle. Organizations that create psychological safety around failure create the conditions for genuine innovation. Organizations that punish failure teach people to avoid risk, which means they also avoid growth.

The US Army's Resilience Training

My son served in the United States Army. What I watched him develop through that service — the resilience, the capacity to operate under pressure, the ability to fail at a task and return to it with greater determination rather than diminished confidence — was built through systematic training in exactly these principles.

Resilience is not a trait you either have or you do not. It is a practice. It is developed through intentional exposure to challenge, followed by honest reflection on what happened and what to do differently.

Reflect: *What is the most significant failure of your recent past? What did you learn from it? And are you applying that learning — or are you still carrying the failure without extracting its value?*

Every failure you are honest about, every setback you learn from, every mistake you do not hide — these are not marks against your record. They are the evidence that you are in the arena, trying, growing, becoming.

CHAPTER 37

Seeking Enlightening Feedback for Growth

John Maxwell once said: Feedback is the breakfast of champions.

I love that image. Because breakfast is not glamorous. It is not the dramatic meal of the day. But without it, nothing else works properly.

Feedback is like that. Unglamorous. Sometimes uncomfortable. Absolutely essential.

What Makes Feedback Actually Useful

Not all feedback is created equal. The most useful feedback is specific, honest, and offered by someone who genuinely understands what you are trying to accomplish and cares about helping you accomplish it.

The least useful feedback is vague, harsh, or offered by someone who has their own agenda. Not all criticism deserves the same weight. Part of the maturity of leadership is developing the judgment to distinguish between feedback that sharpens you and noise that distracts you.

Building the Capacity to Receive

Most of us are better at giving feedback than receiving it. Receiving feedback — really receiving it, without defensiveness, without immediately explaining why the feedback-giver does not understand the full situation — is one of the harder forms of humility.

It is also one of the most important skills in a leader's toolkit.

I have actively sought feedback throughout my career — from mentors, from peers, from team members, from people who disagreed with me. Not all of it was comfortable. Some of it required me to sit with discomfort for a while before I could see its value.

But the feedback that was hardest to hear was often the feedback that changed me most.

> *Reflect:* Is there feedback you have been given recently that you dismissed too quickly? What might you find if you returned to it with more openness?

Seeking feedback is not a sign of weakness. It is a sign of confidence — the confidence that you can handle the truth, and that the truth will make you better.

CHAPTER 38

Persistence and the Richness of Long-Term Payoffs

President Calvin Coolidge once wrote something that I have carried with me for many years: persistence is the one quality that nothing in the world can replace. Talent alone is not enough — there are plenty of talented people who never accomplish what they are capable of. Intelligence alone is not enough — the world is full of educated people who gave up too soon. Only persistence and resolve are, in his words, omnipotent.

I believe that. I have lived it.

The Long Game

J.K. Rowling was rejected by twelve publishers before Harry Potter was accepted. She was a single mother, living on government assistance, writing in cafés. She could have stopped at any point and no one would have blamed her. She did not stop.

I think about that story not because it is dramatic, but because of what it says about time. The payoff, when it came, was not just the books. It was the person she had become through the persistence — the clarity, the discipline, the unshakeable belief in her story.

That is always the deepest payoff of the long game: not just what you achieve, but who you become in the achieving.

Integrity Under the Long Pressure

The hardest thing about persistence is not the effort. It is maintaining your integrity through the long stretches when the results are not visible and the temptations to shortcut are strongest.

I spent seven years in a job where my supervisor was actively working against me. Seven years of doing good work without recognition. Seven years of choosing integrity when compromise would have been easier. The payoff was not immediate. But when it finally came — in the form of a recommendation from the very man who had tried to hold me back — it was clear.

The people who watch you persist with integrity, even when it costs you, never fully forget what they saw. That witness becomes your reputation. And your reputation becomes your legacy.

To the Next Generation

I write these final pages thinking about my sons. About the children of the volunteers I have served. About the young professionals I coach and the future leaders I meet in workshops.

My message to them is the same as the one I have tried to live: where you start does not determine where you lead. The family you were born into, the country you came from, the resources you had or did not have — none of that is the final word on who you become.

What is the final word is your character. Your commitment. Your willingness to persist with integrity through the long, unobserved stretches when no one is applauding.

Be Good. Do Good. Do Well.

That is the whole of it.

— Gopu Shrestha

Blaine, Minnesota

References

Arbinger Institute. (2010). Leadership and self-deception: Getting out of the box (2nd ed.). Berrett-Koehler Publishers.

Bennis, W. (2009). On becoming a leader (4th ed.). Basic Books.

Brown, B. (2010). The gifts of imperfection: Let go of who you think you're supposed to be and embrace who you are. Hazelden Publishing.

Brown, B. (2018). Dare to lead: Brave work, tough conversations, whole hearts. Random House.

Clear, J. (2018). Atomic habits: An easy & proven way to build good habits & break bad ones. Avery.

Collins, J. (2001). Good to great: Why some companies make the leap and others don't. HarperBusiness.

Covey, S. R. (1989). The 7 habits of highly effective people: Powerful lessons in personal change. Free Press.

Duckworth, A. (2016). Grit: The power of passion and perseverance. Scribner.

Dweck, C. S. (2006). Mindset: The new psychology of success. Random House.

Frankl, V. E. (1959). Man's search for meaning. Beacon Press.

Goleman, D., Boyatzis, R., & McKee, A. (2002). Primal leadership: Realizing the power of emotional intelligence. Harvard Business Review Press.

Grenny, J., Patterson, K., McMillan, R., & Switzler, A. (2011). Crucial conversations: Tools for talking when stakes are high (2nd ed.). McGraw-Hill.

Lencioni, P. (2002). The five dysfunctions of a team: A leadership fable. Jossey-Bass.

Maxwell, J. C. (1998). The 21 irrefutable laws of leadership: Follow them and people will follow you. Thomas Nelson.

Maxwell, J. C. (2011). The 5 levels of leadership: Proven steps to maximize your potential. Center Street.

Pink, D. H. (2009). Drive: The surprising truth about what motivates us. Riverhead Books.

Roberts, A. (2019). Leadership in war: Essential lessons from those who made history. Viking.

Sinek, S. (2009). Start with why: How great leaders inspire everyone to take action. Portfolio/Penguin.

Sinek, S. (2014). Leaders eat last: Why some teams pull together and others don't. Portfolio/Penguin.

Willink, J., & Babin, L. (2015). Extreme ownership: How U.S. Navy SEALs lead and win. St. Martin's Press.

Wiseman, L., & McKeown, G. (2010). Multipliers: How the best leaders make everyone smarter. HarperBusiness.

About the Author

Gopu Shrestha grew up in a village in rural Nepal without electricity, running water, or paved roads. With nothing but a secondary school education, a borrowed sum to learn typing, and an unshakeable belief in the power of integrity, he remade his life — rising from site clerk to Finance Director, earning three master's degrees along the way, and eventually becoming a Senior Agile Coach and technology leader serving Fortune 100 companies across America.

He has led Toastmasters District 106 as District Director, serving more than 2,000 volunteers across multiple states and earning the prestigious President's Distinguished District award from World Headquarters. He is also a PhD candidate, a leadership speaker, and the author of Strategic Honesty and You Still Matter.

As a father, Gopu is most proud of his two sons — one a United States Army veteran, one an Environmental Engineer — both of whom he considers living proof of his central teaching: that integrity, persistence, and purpose produce lives worth living.

Gopu speaks and writes under his personal brand, strategichonesty.com, and works with leaders, families, and organizations who want to lead with character rather than just competence.

strategichonesty.com

www.ingramcontent.com/pod-product-compliance
Lightning Source LLC
Chambersburg PA
CBHW050232230526
45470CB00005B/1908